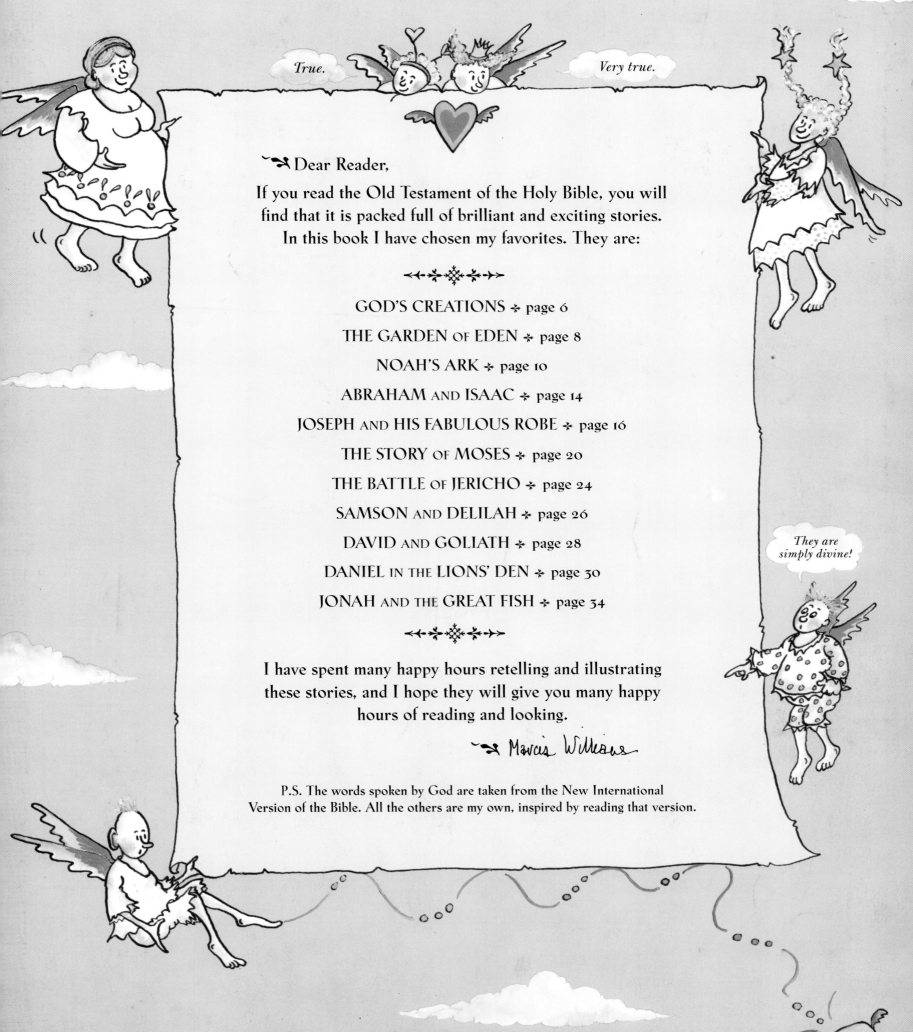

True.

Very true.

Dear Reader,

If you read the Old Testament of the Holy Bible, you will find that it is packed full of brilliant and exciting stories. In this book I have chosen my favorites. They are:

I have spent many happy hours retelling and illustrating these stories, and I hope they will give you many happy hours of reading and looking.

Marcia Williams

They are simply divine!

P.S. The words spoken by God are taken from the New International Version of the Bible. All the others are my own, inspired by reading that version.

First U.S. edition 2004

Library of Congress Cataloging-in-Publication Data
Williams, Marcia, date.
God and his creations : tales from the Old Testament / retold and
illustrated by Marcia Williams. — 1st U.S. ed.

p. cm.

Summary: Retells eleven Old Testament stories in comic book format.
Contents: God's creations — The Garden of Eden — Noah's ark — Abraham and Isaac — Joseph and his fabulous
robe — The story of Moses — The Battle of Jericho and the promised land — Samson and Delilah — David and
Goliath — Daniel in the lions' den — Jonah and the great fish.
ISBN 0-7636-2211-7
1. Bible stories, English—O.T. [1. Bible stories—O.T.—Cartoons and comics. 2. Cartoons and comics.] I. Title.
BS551.3.W55 2004
221.9'505—dc22   2003055339

10 9 8 7 6 5 4 3 2 1

Printed in China

This book was typeset in Phaistos Bold.
The illustrations were done in watercolor and ink.

Candlewick Press
2067 Massachusetts Avenue
Cambridge, Massachusetts 02140

visit us at www.candlewick.com

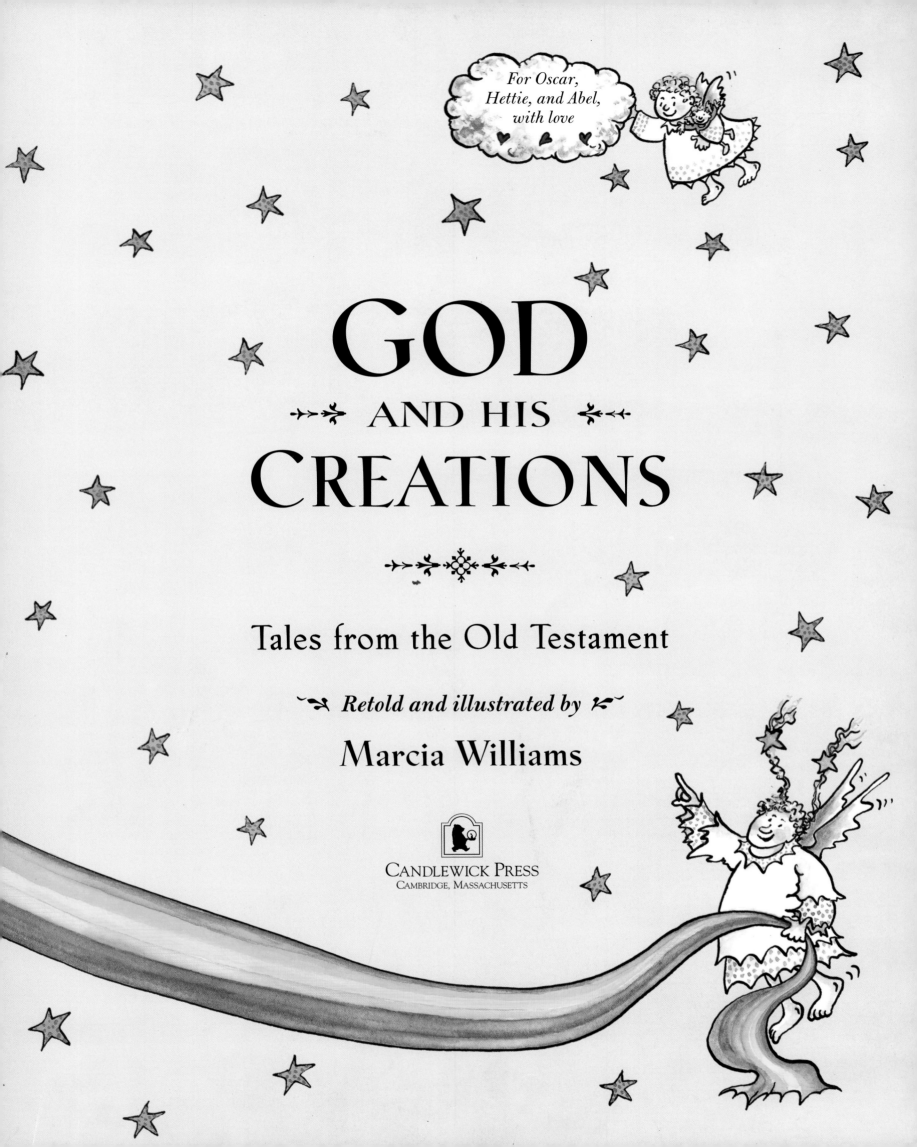

For Oscar,
Hettie, and Abel,
with love

GOD
❖ AND HIS ❖
CREATIONS

Tales from the Old Testament

❖ Retold and illustrated by ❖

Marcia Williams

CANDLEWICK PRESS
CAMBRIDGE, MASSACHUSETTS

Don't forget us, the angels.

Ouch! My toe!

GOD'S CREATIONS

LET

THERE BE

LIGHT!

God's feet (as seen for the first time).

In the beginning there was only God. The earth was formless and dark.

Look, it's me!

DAY!

NIGHT!

DAY!

NIGHT!

Then God created light! He called the light DAY, and the darkness NIGHT — on that first day.

SKY!

On the second day God created space to divide the waters. He called it SKY.

He's on a roll!

RIVERS!   SEAS!   LAND!   PLANTS AND TREES!

On the third day God made RIVERS, SEAS, and dry LAND that was rich in plants and trees.

THIS IS ALL . . .   VERY GOOD!

Pretty!

On the fourth day God put the sun, the moon, and the stars in the sky.
So there was evening, and there was morning.

Wow! An orb ball.

On the fifth day God filled the seas with fish, and the sky with insects and birds.
He loved each and every one.

On the sixth day God was very busy.
He made animals of every shape and size to live upon the land.

Then, out of the dust of the earth, God made men and women.
He made them to care for the earth and for all living creatures.

God saw all that He had made, and it was very good. In six days He had created
the whole world, so He made the seventh day a rest day.

Genesis

THE GARDEN OF EDEN

The first man God breathed life into was Adam. God planted a garden called Eden for Adam to live in. God told Adam to enjoy all the fruits of Eden except for those from the tree of the knowledge of good and evil—for if he tasted these, he would die. Adam obeyed God, for he loved Him. But when God was not with him in the garden, Adam felt lonely.

So while Adam slept, God took a rib from his side.

From the rib of Adam, God made the first woman, Eve.

For some time Adam and Eve lived contentedly in Eden.

But a crafty serpent spoke to Eve beside the tree of knowledge.

He told her that its fruit would make her as wise as God.

So Eve took fruit from the tree of knowledge and ate it.

Then she gave some fruit to Adam, and he ate it.

At once they became ashamed of their nakedness.

God angrily condemned the serpent to crawl upon his belly.

He cast Adam and Eve out of Eden and sent an angel to guard the gate. From then on Adam and Eve had to fend for themselves, where thorns and thistles grew and animals were savage. God still cared for them and the many children born to them. But as He had predicted, Adam and Eve did eventually die—although not until they were very, very old.

Genesis

Then God told Noah to fill the ark with a male and female of every living creature. So he and his family chased, herded, and coaxed until the ark was loaded. As the first drops of rain began to fall, God slammed the great door shut and bolted it firmly.

The rain poured down and the waters rose. The loaded ark was lifted above the earth. Soon no other creatures were left alive, and the highest mountain was covered with water.

For forty days and forty nights the rain fell. The ark floated on the swirling waters.

Thank God it's stopped raining!

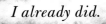

I already did.

Until at last God sent a wind over the earth. The rain ceased, and the waters began to recede.

The ark came to rest on Mt. Ararat. Noah let out a raven, but it found nowhere to land.

A few days later Noah sent out a dove. It flew for miles but could find nowhere to rest its feet.

Seven days later Noah sent out the dove again. In the evening it returned with an olive branch.

After another seven days the dove flew out again. It did not return because the earth had dried.

Their hay days are over.

Noah opened the great doors of the ark, and out rushed his family and all God's creatures. Noah built an altar to thank God, and God was delighted. He promised Noah never to flood the world again, and He set a rainbow in the sky as a sign of His promise.

Genesis

What a wet tale.

Handy things, umbrellas!

ABRAHAM AND ISAAC

After Noah, there was a shepherd named Abraham who loved God above all else. When God asked him to travel to Canaan with his wife, Sarah, he did not hesitate.

When they reached Canaan, God visited them again.

He told Abraham and Sarah that they would have a son.

They laughed, thinking they were too old to have a child.

But the next year, as God had said, Sarah gave birth to a boy.

They named him Isaac, and he grew healthy and strong.

Abraham and Sarah were very proud. They loved Isaac dearly.

So when God asked Abraham to sacrifice Isaac as a burnt offering, Abraham thought his heart would break. But he collected wood, some fire, and a sacrificial knife and set out with his son.

God doesn't do jokes.

Huh! He's only losing a son. I lost my wings!

Oh dear.

JOSEPH AND HIS FABULOUS ROBE

I remember when you were a boy, Isaac.

Dad, Gramps, I've brought the boys to see you.

Isaac, the son of Abraham, stayed in Canaan and had twin sons of his own, Esau and Jacob. Jacob became a farmer and had twelve sons.

That's my boy!

It's cool! Thanks, Dad.

It stinks!

Jacob loved his sons, but especially Joseph. He gave him a new robe. Joseph's brothers were jealous and began to hate him.

Then Joseph had two strange dreams. In the first, Joseph and his brothers were binding corn.

Suddenly Joseph's sheaf rose and stood upright, and his brothers' sheaves bowed down before it.

In the second dream the sun, the moon, and eleven stars bowed down before him as though he were king.

We must keep this matter in mind, my dearest boy!

He thinks he'll actually rule us. Not a chance.

Baa!

His father believed the dreams meant that Joseph would become a ruler. His brothers' hatred grew. They stormed off to tend the sheep.

16

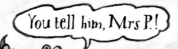

You tell him, Mrs P.!

God likes long-term plans.

In Egypt Joseph was sold as a slave to Potiphar, the captain of Pharaoh's guard.

You are promoted. You now care for the whole household!

Great!

For a while Joseph did well as a slave.

You may please Potiphar, but you don't please me.

Big mistake!

But then Potiphar's wife had him thrown into prison.

Joseph, what do dead rats dream about?

God knows!

In prison Joseph became a wise interpreter of dreams.

God will help Joseph.

Bring that Joseph fellow.

Okay, mighty Pharaoh.

You stink!

You stink to high heaven!

Can you help?

God willing.

So when Pharaoh had two strange dreams, he called upon Joseph to interpret them.

Those are bad dreams!

In the first dream, seven sleek, fat cows came out of the River Nile, followed by seven scrawny, gaunt cows. The scrawny, gaunt cows ate the sleek, fat cows but remained thin.

Grrr!

Crunch!

Help!

Slurp!

Burp!

Fat is not fun!

In his second dream, seven shriveled ears of corn swallowed up seven fat ears of corn.

This matter is firmly decided. Listen!

You must collect grain during the seven good years.

Joseph told Pharaoh that God had sent him a warning: seven years of plenty would be followed by seven years of famine!

Since God has made this known to you, you're in charge.

He needs a haircut.

Great!

Pharaoh was so impressed by Joseph's wisdom that he put him in charge of storing food for the famine to come.

Famine is forbidden in heaven.

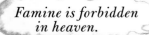

Luckily for you!

Pharaoh gave Joseph many treasures and made him governor of all Egypt.

There were seven years of abundance before the terrible famine struck across many lands. During these years Joseph built storehouses and filled them with vast mounds of grain.

When the famine came, there was grain only in Egypt, and Joseph's brothers traveled there all the way from Canaan to buy food. They did not recognize Joseph, but he recognized them immediately.

Joseph decided to test his brothers, to see if they were still wicked. He threatened to enslave Benjamin, the youngest. The brothers knew how much this would upset their father, and so they pleaded to be enslaved instead. Joseph saw by this that his brothers had changed.

With great joy he made himself known to them. He bade them fetch his father, Jacob, and settle in Egypt.

The Egyptians and Joseph's family all survived the famine — thanks to God, who had brought Joseph to Egypt.

Genesis

19

Trouble comes next, O Israel.

Your name will be Israel.

A new name at my age? What next!

Before Jacob died, God changed his name to Israel, and his descendants—Joseph and his brothers, and their children, and their children's children—became known as the Israelites.

The Israelites have become too numerous. Make them slaves.

Good plan, mighty Pharaoh.

When they give birth, if it's a boy, kill him!

Even better plan, mighty Pharaoh.

The Israelites became so rich and numerous in Egypt that the Pharaoh began to fear their power. He made them slaves and ordered the death of all their baby boys.

Poor, lonely baby.

This must be an Israelite baby.

To save her son, one Israelite mother hid her baby among the reeds by the bank of the Nile. Pharaoh's daughter found him there when she came to bathe. She named the baby Moses and took him home to live with her as her son.

Yummy fish!

Carry the whole pyramid, not just one brick!

Stop that.

Run, Moses, or Daddy will kill you!

I'm out of here!

God must have plans for Moses.

Moses knew that his parents were Israelites, and as he grew older, he tried to protect other Israelites. One day he killed an Egyptian for giving an Israelite slave a cruel beating, and so he was forced to flee from Egypt.

Know-it-all!

I hope his luck holds out.

Far away from Pharaoh's wrath Moses found work as a shepherd. But God had a job for him.

One day God spoke to Moses from a burning bush. He told Moses to lead the Israelites from Egypt into a better land. But Moses was afraid that this task would be too difficult for him.

God told Moses to throw down his staff. It became a snake.

When God told Moses to pick the snake up by the tail, it became a staff again.

God told Moses to put his hand inside his cloak. His hand turned sickly white.

When he replaced his hand inside his cloak, it was healed.

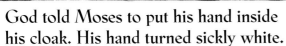

God said signs like these would convince Pharaoh to let the Israelites go. He told Moses not to be afraid. At last Moses obeyed and set out for Egypt with the staff of God in his hand.

Drat, drat, drat, drat!

Yoo-hoo! Moses, I've made a map!

Goal!

21

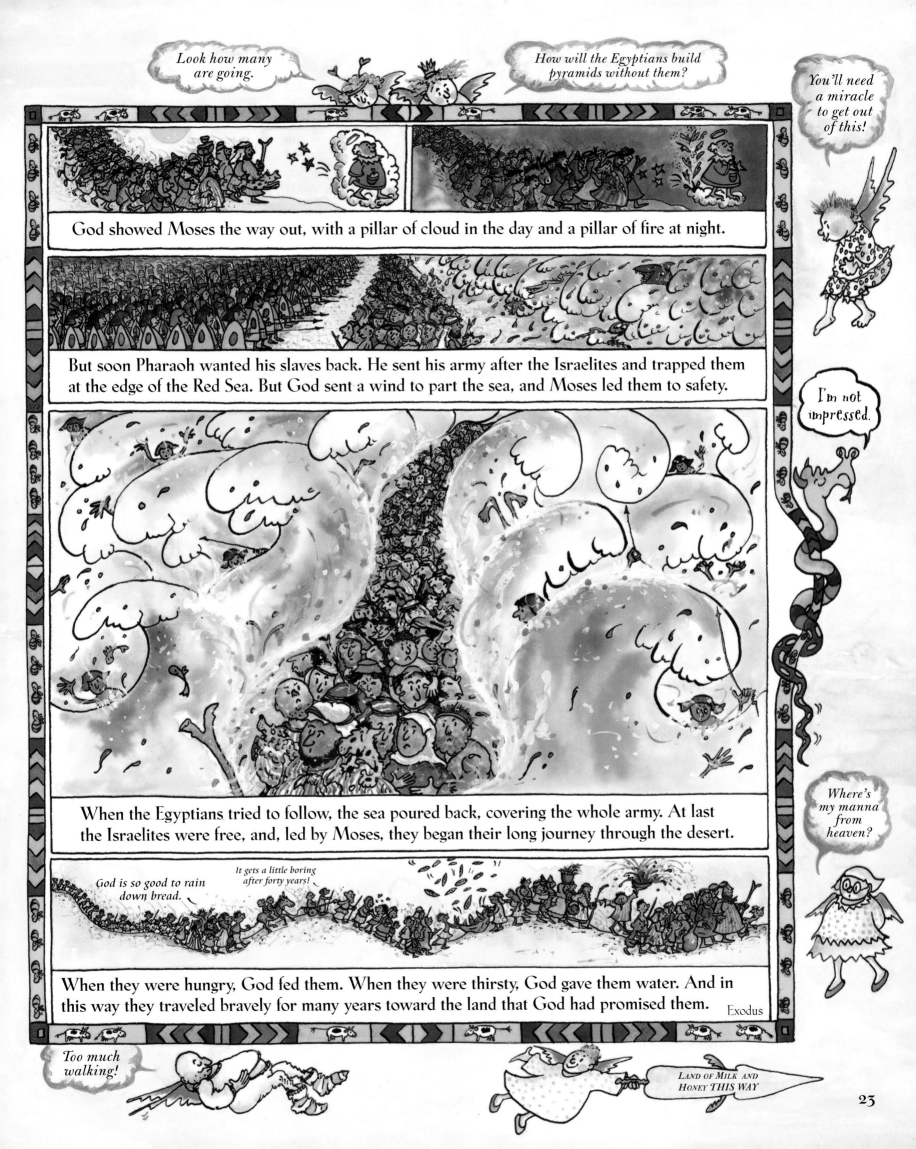

God showed Moses the way out, with a pillar of cloud in the day and a pillar of fire at night.

But soon Pharaoh wanted his slaves back. He sent his army after the Israelites and trapped them at the edge of the Red Sea. But God sent a wind to part the sea, and Moses led them to safety.

When the Egyptians tried to follow, the sea poured back, covering the whole army. At last the Israelites were free, and, led by Moses, they began their long journey through the desert.

When they were hungry, God fed them. When they were thirsty, God gave them water. And in this way they traveled bravely for many years toward the land that God had promised them. Exodus

THE BATTLE OF JERICHO

It's so exciting— they've reached their land.

Take a deep breath before you shout.

THE LORD'S ARMY

By the time the Israelites reached the River Jordan, Moses was too old to travel farther. So God gave them a new leader, a soldier named Joshua. God sent an angel to tell Joshua how to destroy the city of Jericho, which stood between the Israelites and their Promised Land. Once a day for six days Joshua marched his army in silence around the walls of Jericho. Seven priests went with them, sounding their trumpets and carrying the golden ark that held the ten commandments that God had given to Moses.

They say soldiers starve on army rations.

24

On the seventh day the procession marched around the closed city seven times. On the seventh time, when the priests gave one long trumpet blast, the soldiers all gave a great war cry—and the walls of Jericho collapsed before them. Then the soldiers charged in and burned the whole city and everything in it. God was with Joshua and the Israelites that day, and their fame spread far and wide. Now they were free to live in the land He had promised to Moses so long ago.

Joshua

After the fall of Jericho, the Israelites settled in the Promised Land. But they had to fight to keep it, and sometimes they lost and were ruled over by other nations, such as the Philistines.

But God sent numerous leaders to help the Israelites. And the strongest was Samson. He once killed a thousand Philistine soldiers with just the jawbone of a donkey.

The Philistines feared Samson and wanted to know how he could be subdued, so they bribed Delilah, his love, to find out.

Delilah cajoled Samson into telling her that being tied by seven green thongs would weaken him—but it did not.

After more cajoling, Samson said that weaving his hair would weaken him—but it did not.

Delilah became so angry that Samson decided he had better tell her the truth!

That night a Philistine shaved Samson's head. As his hair fell about the bed, his strength left him.

The cruel Philistines blinded Samson and set him to work in a lonely prison.

Months later, the Philistine rulers gathered in their temple and called for Samson. They planned to taunt him. But Samson's hair had grown again, and he asked the jailer to stand him near two pillars. Calling upon God's help, he pushed against the pillars with all his might until the temple came down, burying all the people in it. And so Samson died with his enemies.

Judges

27

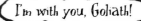

DAVID AND GOLIATH

They have rejected me as their king.

We need a proper king to fight the Philistines.

Me, I'm the tallest.

Okay—Saul for king! Long live King Saul!

The Israelites had many leaders, but no king except God. Until they crowned Saul.

Forward march . . . HALT!

Behold! An Israelite gnome!

King Saul was to help them fight the Philistines and their giant warrior, Goliath.

Fat chance.

Kill me and we will be your subjects.

The fearful Goliath challenged King Saul to find a soldier to fight him in single combat.

I will give great wealth to the man who kills him— great, great wealth— great, great, great wealth.

King Saul offered many fine rewards, but no Israelite dared to fight the giant.

Come on, you wimps!

For forty days and forty nights Goliath took his stand, but still no soldier volunteered.

Big bully!

Who is he to defy the armies of the living God?

Cowards!

David, a shepherd boy, heard Goliath's challenge while he was taking food to his soldier brothers.

I will go and fight him.

You?!

God will deliver me.

Oh well, if you say so.

David was enraged. Goliath's challenge was an insult to God. So he offered to fight.

David loves God.

He puts us to shame.

He's so brave.

Such an honor.

Although David was only a boy, King Saul gave him his own armor and sent him forth.

Thanks so much . . .

but I'm not used to armor.

David found the armor too heavy and threw it off.

That's why he's fighting.

Did his brothers eat the food?

Instead he chose five smooth stones from a stream.

Then, with only his sling, he turned to meet the giant.

Goliath scoffed at the puny size of his enemy.

Goliath began to move closer. David fitted a stone to his sling and hurled it at the giant. The stone sank deep into Goliath's forehead, and he fell to the ground! With a roar of triumph the Israelites chased the terrified Philistines from their land. King Saul realized that God favored David. He decided to keep him at his court. And, after many more adventures, David eventually became king.

Samuel

DANIEL IN THE LIONS' DEN

Daniel was an Israelite from a noble family. When the Babylonians besieged the city of Jerusalem, they seized treasure and took Daniel and three other young nobles to Babylon to serve their king. The Babylonians did not believe in God. They honored their own gods and goddesses.

Daniel and his friends were offered rich food and wine.

But they kept God's law and ate only simple food.

They were wise young men and soon became royal counselors.

God had made Daniel the wisest.

So King Darius made him a state governor.

The Babylonian nobles were outraged!

They plotted to dishonor Daniel.

They persuaded the king to say that everyone had to worship him or else be fed to the lions.

As the Babylonian nobles had hoped, Daniel would worship only his own God.

The delighted nobles rushed to inform the king and demand Daniel's punishment.

King Darius loved Daniel, but he had to uphold the law of his kingdom. Daniel was thrown into the lions' den. King Darius spent a sleepless night, imagining his friend being eaten by the lions.

At the first light of dawn he ran to the den and called out to Daniel. To his amazement, Daniel answered. With the help of an angel, God had shut the mouths of the lions.

The king was overjoyed and declared that all Babylonians should now honor the God of Daniel. The nobles were not pleased.

JONAH AND THE GREAT FISH

Go to the great city of Nineveh and preach against it.

Nineveh . . . me? You're joking? You're not joking!

I'd go to Nineveh for you!

Too high again.

God wanted people to be kind. When they were cruel, he tried to change their ways. He once asked the prophet Jonah to go to Nineveh in Assyria and warn the people against their wickedness.

Ahoy, hold hard, heave over . . . WAIT!

You'll be in for it now!

Assyria was the land of Israel's enemy, and Jonah did not want to go. He hurried aboard a ship sailing in the opposite direction. This angered God!

So God sent a terrifying storm that threatened to break up the ship. The wind tore at its sails, and the waves crashed against its hull. The ship shuddered and creaked.

He is seriously angry.

Ssplendid! A disobedient prophet.

34

Jonah prayed to God, but the waves grew taller and more violent. Jonah told the sailors that God had sent the storm because he had not obeyed Him.

Jonah asked the sailors to throw him into the sea. Then God would calm the waters. But they did not want to drown Jonah, so they tried hard to row to land. But the sea was too wild.

Eventually the sailors were forced to throw Jonah overboard. The waters grew calm.

While the sailors rowed toward land, Jonah sank beneath the surface of the sea.

Jonah did not drown because God sent a great fish to swallow him. He stayed inside the belly of the fish for three days and three nights, praying for God's forgiveness.

Then God told the fish to vomit Jonah out onto dry land. God again asked Jonah to go to Nineveh and warn the people against their wickedness. This time Jonah went!

In Nineveh, Jonah warned the people that God would destroy their city unless they repented.

The king and the Ninevites believed Jonah. They put on sackcloth and turned their backs on evil.

When God saw that Jonah had changed the minds of the Ninevites, He decided to spare Nineveh. Everyone rejoiced and praised God. And God was happy with His creations.

Jonah